Password Logbook

_____

_____

_____

Passwords

🌐 WEBSITE

👤 USERNAME

✉ EMAIL

***** PASSWORD

📝 NOTES

🌐 WEBSITE

👤 USERNAME

✉ EMAIL

***** PASSWORD

📝 NOTES

🌐 WEBSITE

👤 USERNAME

✉ EMAIL

***** PASSWORD

📝 NOTES

🌐 WEBSITE

👤 USERNAME

✉ EMAIL

***** PASSWORD

📝 NOTES

🌐

👤

✉

*****

📝

🌐

👤

✉

*****

📝

🌐

👤

✉

*****

📝

🌐

👤

✉

*****

📝

PASSWORDS

🌐 WEBSITE

👤 USERNAME

@ EMAIL

***** PASSWORD

📝 NOTES

🌐 WEBSITE

👤 USERNAME

@ EMAIL

***** PASSWORD

📝 NOTES

🌐

👤

@

*****

📝

🌐

👤

@

*****

📝

🌐

👤

@

*****

📝

🌐

👤

@

*****

📝

PASSWORDS

WEBSITE

Username _____

Email _____

Password _____

Notes

WEBSITE

Username _____

Email _____

Password _____

Notes

Passwords

🌐 Website

👤 Username
_____

@ Email
_____

***** Password
_____

📝 Notes

🌐 Website

👤 Username
_____

@ Email
_____

***** Password
_____

📝 Notes

🌐 _____   🌐 _____

👤 _____   👤 _____

@ _____   @ _____

***** _____   ***** _____

📝   📝

🌐 _____   🌐 _____

👤 _____   👤 _____

@ _____   @ _____

***** _____   ***** _____

📝   📝

PASSWORDS

🌐 WEBSITE

👤 USERNAME

✉ EMAIL

••••• PASSWORD

📝 NOTES

🌐 WEBSITE

👤 USERNAME

✉ EMAIL

••••• PASSWORD

📝 NOTES

🌐

👤

✉

•••••

📝

🌐

👤

✉

•••••

📝

🌐

👤

✉

•••••

📝

🌐

👤

✉

•••••

📝

Passwords

WEBSITE

USERNAME

EMAIL

PASSWORD

NOTES

WEBSITE

USERNAME

EMAIL

PASSWORD

NOTES

PASSWORDS

WEBSITE

USERNAME

EMAIL

PASSWORD

NOTES

WEBSITE

USERNAME

EMAIL

PASSWORD

NOTES

PASSWORDS

WEBSITE

USERNAME

EMAIL

PASSWORD

NOTES

WEBSITE

USERNAME

EMAIL

PASSWORD

NOTES

PASSWORDS

🌐 WEBSITE
- 👤 USERNAME
- ✉ EMAIL
- ***** PASSWORD
- 📝 NOTES

🌐 WEBSITE
- 👤 USERNAME
- ✉ EMAIL
- ***** PASSWORD
- 📝 NOTES

PASSWORDS

🌐 WEBSITE

👤 USERNAME

✉ EMAIL

🔑 PASSWORD

📝 NOTES

🌐 WEBSITE

👤 USERNAME

✉ EMAIL

🔑 PASSWORD

📝 NOTES

PASSWORDS

WEBSITE

Username

Email

Password

Notes

WEBSITE

Username

Email

Password

Notes

PASSWORDS

WEBSITE

USERNAME

EMAIL

PASSWORD

NOTES

WEBSITE

USERNAME

EMAIL

PASSWORD

NOTES

PASSWORDS

WEBSITE

USERNAME

EMAIL

PASSWORD

NOTES

WEBSITE

USERNAME

EMAIL

PASSWORD

NOTES

PASSWORDS

WEBSITE

USERNAME

EMAIL

PASSWORD

NOTES

WEBSITE

USERNAME

EMAIL

PASSWORD

NOTES

PASSWORDS

WEBSITE

USERNAME _____

EMAIL _____

PASSWORD _____

NOTES _____

WEBSITE

USERNAME _____

EMAIL _____

PASSWORD _____

NOTES _____

PASSWORDS

WEBSITE

USERNAME

EMAIL

PASSWORD

NOTES

WEBSITE

USERNAME

EMAIL

PASSWORD

NOTES

PASSWORDS

WEBSITE

USERNAME

EMAIL

PASSWORD

NOTES

WEBSITE

USERNAME

EMAIL

PASSWORD

NOTES

🌐 WEBSITE

👤 USERNAME

✉@ EMAIL

***** PASSWORD

📝 NOTES

🌐 WEBSITE

👤 USERNAME

✉@ EMAIL

***** PASSWORD

📝 NOTES

PASSWORDS

WEBSITE

USERNAME

EMAIL

PASSWORD

NOTES

WEBSITE

USERNAME

EMAIL

PASSWORD

NOTES

PASSWORDS

🌐 **WEBSITE**

👤 USERNAME

✉ EMAIL

***** PASSWORD

📝 NOTES

🌐 **WEBSITE**

👤 USERNAME

✉ EMAIL

***** PASSWORD

📝 NOTES

🌐

👤

✉

*****

📝

🌐

👤

✉

*****

📝

🌐

👤

✉

*****

📝

🌐

👤

✉

*****

📝

Passwords

🌐 WEBSITE

👤 USERNAME

✉ EMAIL

***** PASSWORD

📝 NOTES

🌐 WEBSITE

👤 USERNAME

✉ EMAIL

***** PASSWORD

📝 NOTES

🌐

👤

✉

*****

📝

🌐

👤

✉

*****

📝

🌐

👤

✉

*****

📝

🌐

👤

✉

*****

📝

Passwords

WEBSITE

USERNAME

EMAIL

PASSWORD

NOTES

WEBSITE

USERNAME

EMAIL

PASSWORD

NOTES

PASSWORDS

🌐 WEBSITE

👤 USERNAME

✉ EMAIL

🔒 PASSWORD

📝 NOTES

🌐 WEBSITE

👤 USERNAME

✉ EMAIL

🔒 PASSWORD

📝 NOTES

Passwords

🌐 Website

👤 Username _____

✉ Email _____

***** Password _____

📝 Notes _____

🌐 Website

👤 Username _____

✉ Email _____

***** Password _____

📝 Notes _____

🌐 _____

👤 _____

✉ _____

***** _____

📝

🌐 _____

👤 _____

✉ _____

***** _____

📝

🌐 _____

👤 _____

✉ _____

***** _____

📝

🌐 _____

👤 _____

✉ _____

***** _____

📝

PASSWORDS

WEBSITE

Ⓐ USERNAME

✉ EMAIL

***** PASSWORD

📝 NOTES

WEBSITE

Ⓐ USERNAME

✉ EMAIL

***** PASSWORD

📝 NOTES

PASSWORDS

WEBSITE

USERNAME

EMAIL

PASSWORD

NOTES

WEBSITE

USERNAME

EMAIL

PASSWORD

NOTES

PASSWORDS

WEBSITE

USERNAME

EMAIL

PASSWORD

NOTES

WEBSITE

USERNAME

EMAIL

PASSWORD

NOTES

PASSWORDS

WEBSITE

USERNAME

EMAIL

PASSWORD

NOTES

WEBSITE

USERNAME

EMAIL

PASSWORD

NOTES

PASSWORDS

WEBSITE

USERNAME

EMAIL

PASSWORD

NOTES

WEBSITE

USERNAME

EMAIL

PASSWORD

NOTES

Passwords

WEBSITE

USERNAME

EMAIL

PASSWORD

NOTES

WEBSITE

USERNAME

EMAIL

PASSWORD

NOTES

PASSWORDS

WEBSITE

Username _____

Email _____

Password _____

Notes

WEBSITE

Username _____

Email _____

Password _____

Notes

PASSWORDS

WEBSITE

USERNAME

EMAIL

PASSWORD

NOTES

WEBSITE

USERNAME

EMAIL

PASSWORD

NOTES

PASSWORDS

WWW WEBSITE

USERNAME

EMAIL

PASSWORD

NOTES

WWW WEBSITE

USERNAME

EMAIL

PASSWORD

NOTES

PASSWORDS

WEBSITE

USERNAME

EMAIL

PASSWORD

NOTES

WEBSITE

USERNAME

EMAIL

PASSWORD

NOTES

PASSWORDS

WEBSITE

USERNAME

EMAIL

PASSWORD

NOTES

WEBSITE

USERNAME

EMAIL

PASSWORD

NOTES

PASSWORDS

🌐 WEBSITE

👤 USERNAME

✉️ EMAIL

🔒 PASSWORD

📝 NOTES

🌐 WEBSITE

👤 USERNAME

✉️ EMAIL

🔒 PASSWORD

📝 NOTES

🌐

👤

✉️

🔒

📝

🌐

👤

✉️

🔒

📝

🌐

👤

✉️

🔒

📝

🌐

👤

✉️

🔒

📝

PASSWORDS

WEBSITE

(Q) USERNAME _____

(@) EMAIL _____

(*****) PASSWORD _____

(📝) NOTES _____

WEBSITE

(Q) USERNAME _____

(@) EMAIL _____

(*****) PASSWORD _____

(📝) NOTES _____

(🌐) _____

(Q) _____

(@) _____

(*****) _____

(📝)

(🌐) _____

(Q) _____

(@) _____

(*****) _____

(📝)

(🌐) _____

(Q) _____

(@) _____

(*****) _____

(📝)

(🌐) _____

(Q) _____

(@) _____

(*****) _____

(📝)

PASSWORDS

WEBSITE

USERNAME

EMAIL

PASSWORD

NOTES

WEBSITE

USERNAME

EMAIL

PASSWORD

NOTES

PASSWORDS

WEBSITE

👤 USERNAME

@ EMAIL

***** PASSWORD

📝 NOTES

WEBSITE

👤 USERNAME

@ EMAIL

***** PASSWORD

📝 NOTES

PASSWORDS

WEBSITE

USERNAME

EMAIL

PASSWORD

NOTES

WEBSITE

USERNAME

EMAIL

PASSWORD

NOTES

PASSWORDS

WEBSITE

Ⓐ USERNAME

@ EMAIL

***** PASSWORD

📝 NOTES

WEBSITE

Ⓐ USERNAME

@ EMAIL

***** PASSWORD

📝 NOTES

PASSWORDS

🌐 WEBSITE

👤 USERNAME

✉ EMAIL

***** PASSWORD

📝 NOTES

🌐 WEBSITE

👤 USERNAME

✉ EMAIL

***** PASSWORD

📝 NOTES

🌐

👤

✉

*****

📝

🌐

👤

✉

*****

📝

🌐

👤

✉

*****

📝

🌐

👤

✉

*****

📝

Passwords

🌐 Website

👤 Username

✉ Email

***** Password

📝 Notes

🌐 Website

👤 Username

✉ Email

***** Password

📝 Notes

🌐

👤

✉

*****

📝

🌐

👤

✉

*****

📝

🌐

👤

✉

*****

📝

🌐

👤

✉

*****

📝

PASSWORDS

🌐 WEBSITE

👤 USERNAME

✉ EMAIL

***** PASSWORD

📝 NOTES

🌐 WEBSITE

👤 USERNAME

✉ EMAIL

***** PASSWORD

📝 NOTES

🌐

👤

✉

*****

📝

🌐

👤

✉

*****

📝

🌐

👤

✉

*****

📝

🌐

👤

✉

*****

📝

PASSWORDS

WEBSITE

USERNAME

EMAIL

PASSWORD

NOTES

WEBSITE

USERNAME

EMAIL

PASSWORD

NOTES

PASSWORDS

WWW **WEBSITE**

👤 USERNAME.

@ EMAIL

***** PASSWORD

📝 NOTES

WWW **WEBSITE**

👤 USERNAME

@ EMAIL

***** PASSWORD

📝 NOTES

PASSWORDS

WEBSITE

USERNAME

EMAIL

PASSWORD

NOTES

WEBSITE

USERNAME

EMAIL

PASSWORD

NOTES

Passwords

WEBSITE

USERNAME

EMAIL

PASSWORD

NOTES

WEBSITE

USERNAME

EMAIL

PASSWORD

NOTES

PASSWORDS

🌐 WEBSITE

👤 USERNAME

✉@ EMAIL

***** PASSWORD

📝 NOTES

🌐 WEBSITE

👤 USERNAME

✉@ EMAIL

***** PASSWORD

📝 NOTES

🌐

👤

✉@

*****

📝

🌐

👤

✉@

*****

📝

🌐

👤

✉@

*****

📝

🌐

👤

✉@

*****

📝

PASSWORDS

WEBSITE

👤 USERNAME

@ EMAIL

***** PASSWORD

📝 NOTES

WEBSITE

👤 USERNAME

@ EMAIL

***** PASSWORD

📝 NOTES

PASSWORDS

	WEBSITE

(Q) USERNAME

(@) EMAIL

(*****) PASSWORD

(✎) NOTES

	WEBSITE

(Q) USERNAME

(@) EMAIL

(*****) PASSWORD

(✎) NOTES

PASSWORDS

🌐 **WEBSITE**

👤 USERNAME

@ EMAIL

***** PASSWORD

📝 NOTES

🌐 **WEBSITE**

👤 USERNAME

@ EMAIL

***** PASSWORD

📝 NOTES

🌐

👤

@

*****

📝

🌐

👤

@

*****

📝

🌐

👤

@

*****

📝

🌐

👤

@

*****

📝

PASSWORDS

WEBSITE

USERNAME

EMAIL

PASSWORD

NOTES

WEBSITE

USERNAME

EMAIL

PASSWORD

NOTES

PASSWORDS

WEBSITE

USERNAME

EMAIL

PASSWORD

NOTES

WEBSITE

USERNAME

EMAIL

PASSWORD

NOTES

PASSWORDS

🌐 WEBSITE

👤 USERNAME

✉ EMAIL

***** PASSWORD

📝 NOTES

🌐 WEBSITE

👤 USERNAME

✉ EMAIL

***** PASSWORD

📝 NOTES

🌐

👤

✉

*****

📝

🌐

👤

✉

*****

📝

🌐

👤

✉

*****

📝

🌐

👤

✉

*****

📝

PASSWORDS

WEBSITE

USERNAME

EMAIL

PASSWORD

NOTES

WEBSITE

USERNAME

EMAIL

PASSWORD

NOTES

PASSWORDS

WEBSITE

USERNAME

EMAIL

PASSWORD

NOTES

WEBSITE

USERNAME

EMAIL

PASSWORD

NOTES

Passwords

Website

Username

Email

Password

Notes

Website

Username

Email

Password

Notes

PASSWORDS

WEBSITE

USERNAME

EMAIL

PASSWORD

NOTES

WEBSITE

USERNAME

EMAIL

PASSWORD

NOTES

PASSWORDS

WEBSITE

USERNAME

EMAIL

PASSWORD

NOTES

WEBSITE

USERNAME

EMAIL

PASSWORD

NOTES

PASSWORDS

WEBSITE

USERNAME

EMAIL

PASSWORD

NOTES

WEBSITE

USERNAME

EMAIL

PASSWORD

NOTES

PASSWORDS

WEBSITE

USERNAME

EMAIL

PASSWORD

NOTES

WEBSITE

USERNAME

EMAIL

PASSWORD

NOTES

PASSWORDS

WEBSITE

USERNAME

EMAIL

PASSWORD

NOTES

WEBSITE

USERNAME

EMAIL

PASSWORD

NOTES

PASSWORDS

🌐 WEBSITE

👤 USERNAME

✉ EMAIL

***** PASSWORD

📝 NOTES

🌐 WEBSITE

👤 USERNAME

✉ EMAIL

***** PASSWORD

📝 NOTES

🌐

👤

✉

*****

📝

🌐

👤

✉

*****

📝

🌐

👤

✉

*****

📝

🌐

👤

✉

*****

📝

PASSWORDS

🌐 WEBSITE

👤 USERNAME

@ EMAIL

***** PASSWORD

📝 NOTES

🌐 WEBSITE

👤 USERNAME

@ EMAIL

***** PASSWORD

📝 NOTES

PASSWORDS

WEBSITE

Username _____

Email _____

Password _____

Notes _____

WEBSITE

Username _____

Email _____

Password _____

Notes _____

PASSWORDS

WEBSITE
USERNAME
EMAIL
PASSWORD
NOTES

WEBSITE
USERNAME
EMAIL
PASSWORD
NOTES

PASSWORDS

🌐 WEBSITE

👤 USERNAME

✉ EMAIL

***** PASSWORD

📝 NOTES

🌐 WEBSITE

👤 USERNAME

✉ EMAIL

***** PASSWORD

📝 NOTES

WEBSITE

USERNAME

EMAIL

PASSWORD

NOTES

WEBSITE

USERNAME

EMAIL

PASSWORD

NOTES

Passwords

🌐 Website

👤 Username

✉@ Email

***** Password

📝 Notes

🌐 Website

👤 Username

✉@ Email

***** Password

📝 Notes

PASSWORDS

WEBSITE

USERNAME

EMAIL

PASSWORD

NOTES

WEBSITE

USERNAME

EMAIL

PASSWORD

NOTES

PASSWORDS

WWW WEBSITE

Username _____

Email _____

Password _____

Notes _____

WWW WEBSITE

Username _____

Email _____

Password _____

Notes _____

PASSWORDS

WEBSITE

USERNAME

EMAIL

PASSWORD

NOTES

WEBSITE

USERNAME

EMAIL

PASSWORD

NOTES

PASSWORDS

WEBSITE

USERNAME

EMAIL

PASSWORD

NOTES

WEBSITE

USERNAME

EMAIL

PASSWORD

NOTES

PASSWORDS

WEBSITE

USERNAME

EMAIL

PASSWORD

NOTES

WEBSITE

USERNAME

EMAIL

PASSWORD

NOTES

PASSWORDS

WEBSITE

USERNAME

EMAIL

PASSWORD

NOTES

WEBSITE

USERNAME

EMAIL

PASSWORD

NOTES

PASSWORDS

WEBSITE

⊗ USERNAME

@ EMAIL

***** PASSWORD

NOTES

WEBSITE

⊗ USERNAME

@ EMAIL

***** PASSWORD

NOTES

PASSWORDS

🌐 WEBSITE

👤 USERNAME

@ EMAIL

***** PASSWORD

📝 NOTES

🌐 WEBSITE

👤 USERNAME

@ EMAIL

***** PASSWORD

📝 NOTES

🌐

👤

@

*****

📝

🌐

👤

@

*****

📝

🌐

👤

@

*****

📝

🌐

👤

@

*****

📝

PASSWORDS

WEBSITE

USERNAME

EMAIL

PASSWORD

NOTES

WEBSITE

USERNAME

EMAIL

PASSWORD

NOTES

PASSWORDS

WEBSITE

USERNAME

EMAIL

PASSWORD

NOTES

WEBSITE

USERNAME

EMAIL

PASSWORD

NOTES

PASSWORDS

WEBSITE

USERNAME

EMAIL

PASSWORD

NOTES

WEBSITE

USERNAME

EMAIL

PASSWORD

NOTES

PASSWORDS

WEBSITE

USERNAME

EMAIL

PASSWORD

NOTES

WEBSITE

USERNAME

EMAIL

PASSWORD

NOTES

PASSWORDS

🌐 WEBSITE

👤 USERNAME

✉@ EMAIL

***** PASSWORD

📝 NOTES

🌐 WEBSITE

👤 USERNAME

✉@ EMAIL

***** PASSWORD

📝 NOTES

PASSWORDS

WEBSITE

Ⓡ USERNAME

@ EMAIL

***** PASSWORD

✎ NOTES

WEBSITE

Ⓡ USERNAME

@ EMAIL

***** PASSWORD

✎ NOTES

PASSWORDS

WEBSITE

Ⓐ USERNAME

✉ EMAIL

***** PASSWORD

📝 NOTES

WEBSITE

Ⓐ USERNAME

✉ EMAIL

***** PASSWORD

📝 NOTES

PASSWORDS

WEBSITE

USERNAME

EMAIL

PASSWORD

NOTES

WEBSITE

USERNAME

EMAIL

PASSWORD

NOTES

PASSWORDS

WEBSITE

USERNAME

EMAIL

PASSWORD

NOTES

WEBSITE

USERNAME

EMAIL

PASSWORD

NOTES

PASSWORDS

🌐 WEBSITE

👤 USERNAME

✉ EMAIL

***** PASSWORD

📝 NOTES

🌐 WEBSITE

👤 USERNAME

✉ EMAIL

***** PASSWORD

📝 NOTES

🌐

👤

✉

*****

📝

🌐

👤

✉

*****

📝

🌐

👤

✉

*****

📝

🌐

👤

✉

*****

📝

PASSWORDS

WEBSITE

USERNAME

EMAIL

PASSWORD

NOTES

WEBSITE

USERNAME

EMAIL

PASSWORD

NOTES

Passwords

⊕ WEBSITE

⊖ USERNAME

⊠ EMAIL

⊡ PASSWORD

▱ NOTES

⊕ WEBSITE

⊖ USERNAME

⊠ EMAIL

⊡ PASSWORD

▱ NOTES

⊕

⊖

⊠

⊡

▱

⊕

⊖

⊠

⊡

▱

⊕

⊖

⊠

⊡

▱

⊕

⊖

⊠

⊡

▱

PASSWORDS

WEBSITE

(8) USERNAME

@ EMAIL

(*****) PASSWORD

NOTES

WEBSITE

(8) USERNAME

@ EMAIL

(*****) PASSWORD

NOTES

PASSWORDS

🌐 WEBSITE

👤 USERNAME

@ EMAIL

***** PASSWORD

📝 NOTES

🌐 WEBSITE

👤 USERNAME

@ EMAIL

***** PASSWORD

📝 NOTES

PASSWORDS

WEBSITE

USERNAME

EMAIL

PASSWORD

NOTES

WEBSITE

USERNAME

EMAIL

PASSWORD

NOTES

PASSWORDS

WEBSITE

USERNAME

EMAIL

PASSWORD

NOTES

WEBSITE

USERNAME

EMAIL

PASSWORD

NOTES

PASSWORDS

WEBSITE

USERNAME

EMAIL

PASSWORD

NOTES

WEBSITE

USERNAME

EMAIL

PASSWORD

NOTES

PASSWORDS

WEBSITE

USERNAME

EMAIL

PASSWORD

NOTES

WEBSITE

USERNAME

EMAIL

PASSWORD

NOTES

PASSWORDS

WEBSITE

- USERNAME
- EMAIL
- PASSWORD
- NOTES

WEBSITE

- USERNAME
- EMAIL
- PASSWORD
- NOTES

PASSWORDS

WEBSITE

USERNAME

EMAIL

PASSWORD

NOTES

WEBSITE

USERNAME

EMAIL

PASSWORD

NOTES

PASSWORDS

WEBSITE

USERNAME

EMAIL

PASSWORD

NOTES

WEBSITE

USERNAME

EMAIL

PASSWORD

NOTES

PASSWORDS

WEBSITE

USERNAME

EMAIL

PASSWORD

NOTES

WEBSITE

USERNAME

EMAIL

PASSWORD

NOTES

PASSWORDS

WEBSITE

USERNAME

EMAIL

PASSWORD

NOTES

WEBSITE

USERNAME

EMAIL

PASSWORD

NOTES

PASSWORDS

WEBSITE

♟ USERNAME

✉ EMAIL

⊞ PASSWORD

✎ NOTES

WEBSITE

♟ USERNAME

✉ EMAIL

⊞ PASSWORD

✎ NOTES

PASSWORDS

WEBSITE

USERNAME

EMAIL

PASSWORD

NOTES

WEBSITE

USERNAME

EMAIL

PASSWORD

NOTES

FAVORITE WEBSITES

WEBSITE

USERNAME

EMAIL

PASSWORD

NOTES

WEBSITE

USERNAME

EMAIL

PASSWORD

NOTES

FAVORITE WEBSITES

🌐 WEBSITE

👤 USERNAME

✉ EMAIL

***** PASSWORD

📝 NOTES

🌐 WEBSITE

👤 USERNAME

✉ EMAIL

***** PASSWORD

📝 NOTES

FAVORITE WEBSITES

WEBSITE

USERNAME

EMAIL

PASSWORD

NOTES

WEBSITE

USERNAME

EMAIL

PASSWORD

NOTES

FAVORITE WEBSITES

WEBSITE

USERNAME

EMAIL

PASSWORD

NOTES

WEBSITE

USERNAME

EMAIL

PASSWORD

NOTES

Favorite Websites

🌐 Website
👤 Username _____

✉@ Email _____

***** Password _____

📝 Notes

🌐 Website
👤 Username _____

✉@ Email _____

***** Password _____

📝 Notes

🌐 _____

👤 _____

✉@ _____

***** _____

📝

🌐 _____

👤 _____

✉@ _____

***** _____

📝

🌐 _____

👤 _____

✉@ _____

***** _____

📝

🌐 _____

👤 _____

✉@ _____

***** _____

📝

FAVORITE WEBSITES

WEBSITE

USERNAME

EMAIL

PASSWORD

NOTES

WEBSITE

USERNAME

EMAIL

PASSWORD

NOTES

THANK YOU FOR PURCHASING OUR PASSWORD LOGBOOK!

ALTHOUGH WRITING DOWN PASSWORDS SEEMS OLD-FASHIONED, IT IS A GOOD WAY TO REMEMBER THEM.

IT IS ALSO POSSIBLE TO WRITE ONLY A HINT ABOUT THE PASSWORD AND NOT THE PASSWORD ITSELF.

BUT KEEP IN MIND: HIDE THIS BOOK IN A SAFE PLACE YOU HAVE CONSTANT ACCESS TO.

WE HOPE THAT YOU ARE SATISFIED WITH THIS BOOK.

THE SATISFACTION OF OUR CUSTOMERS IS OUR MAIN FOCUS AND WE WOULD BE HAPPY IF YOU COULD GIVE US YOUR FEEDBACK ABOUT THE LOGBOOK.

IT WOULD BE GREAT IF YOU COULD TAKE THE TIME TO WRITE AN HONEST CUSTOMER REVIEW ON AMAZON. THIS WILL HELP US AND OTHER CUSTOMERS ON AMAZON TO MAKE A BETTER BUYING DECISION.

THANK YOU VERY MUCH!

Made in the USA
Las Vegas, NV
01 December 2024

13017853R00069